NGANAJUNGU YAGU
CHARMAINE PAPERTALK GREEN

Other publications by Charmaine Papertalk Green

POETRY
False Claims of Colonial Thieves (with John Kinsella)
Just Like That
Tiptoeing Tod the Tracker

NGANAJUNGU YAGU

CHARMAINE PAPERTALK GREEN

CorditeBooks

First printed in 2019
by Cordite Publishing Inc.

PO Box 393
Carlton South 3053
Victoria, Australia
cordite.org.au | corditebooks.org.au

National Library of Australia
Cataloguing-in-Publication:

  Papertalk Green, Charmaine
  Nganajungu Yagu
  978-0-6485116-0-1 paperback
  I. Title.
  A821.3

Poetry set in Bembo 10 / 14
Cover design by Zoë Sadokierski
Text design by Kent MacCarter and Zoë Sadokierski
Printed and bound by McPherson's Printing, Maryborough, Victoria.

10 9 8 7 6 5 4 3

for Yagu - Margaret Rose (dec) - Munggu barna woman

CONTENTS

PREFACE

Forty years ago, letters, words and feelings flowed between a teenage daughter and her mother. Letters written by that teenage daughter – me – handed around family back home, disappeared. Yet letters from that mother to her teenage daughter – me – remained protected in my red life-journey suitcase. I carried them across time and landscapes as a mother would carry her baby in a thaga.

In 1978–79, I was living in an Aboriginal girls' hostel in the Bentley suburb of Perth, attending senior high school. Mum and I sent handwritten letters to each other. I was a small-town teenager stepping outside of all things I had ever known. Mum remained in the only world she had ever known.

Nganajungu Yagu was inspired by Mother's letters, her life and the love she instilled in me for my people and my culture. A substantial part of that culture is language, and I missed out on so much language interaction having moved away. I talk with my ancestors' language – Badimaya and Wajarri – to honour ancestors, language centres, language workers and those Yamaji who have been and remain generous in passing on cultural knowledge.

Left: A young Margaret Rose Papertalk, 1949, Geraldton, WA

INTRODUCTION

Since Charmaine Papertalk Green's poetry was first published in *The Penguin Book of Australian Women Poets* in 1986, her voice on the page has been consistent: eloquently powerful, respectfully challenging and true to her role in life as a Yamaji Nyarlu. *Nganajungu Yagu* is no different, considering, as it does, respect for ancestors, connection to country, the role of the poet and Yamaji identity.

The writing in *Nganajungu Yagu* is dedicated to Papertalk Green's mother, and is built around a series of selected correspondence between her and her mother; each provides a deeply personal insight into not only their relationship, but the cultural, political and social landscape of her Yamaji country during the 1970s.

As Papertalk Green writes, these are 'not just letters'. Rather, they create a tangible story and bond between Yagu and Daughter, and gently remind us of the sacrifices made by most of our matriarchs over time. Each letter and response provide not only a 'mark of existence' for the writer but a medium for mother and daughter to connect while at a distance. Her gift is one that makes us pause and reflect on our own behaviours. The love and respect penned here will inspire readers of any age and identity to think about the ways we engage people we love through words. Or, more importantly, the ways we should engage.

The revival of letters here not only reminds me of the nearly lost art of letter-writing, but the impact a letter has on its receiver. 'I could feel the love hugs springing off the paper', she writes in 'Paper Love'. I challenge any reader to put this book down and not feel compelled to write a letter to someone in their life – past or present.

It is through the bilingual poem 'Walgajunmanha All Time' that Papertalk Green clarifies her role as a First Nations writer, and I honour her for keeping our people, our stories and the Yamaji language on the literary radar and accessible to all readers through her poetry. When the academy, the literati and festival directors discuss Australian poetry in the years to come, they should all have *Nganajungu Yagu* on the top of their lists, and Papertalk Green as a key voice in the poetic landscape.

In the United Nations International Year of Indigenous Languages, *Nganajungu Yagu* is a work of cultural significance and educational influence. As I closed this book for the first time, I found myself circling back in my mind to a number of phrases. Those that keep recurring are —

> Yagu, I always remembered the beauty of our culture
> despite the racism seen in every step I took along years
> culture love was and is the anchor for everything done.

—Anita Heiss

Gudiya 1: More Than a Yarn: Thaga

Every Yamaji girl has a red journey suitcase of sort, unna?

I have heard people say that experiences, not things, are more important in a journey. I disagree when reflecting on my red journey suitcase 'thing' … let's just call it RJS. The experiences and emotions that travelled with me and RJS near forty years are what I call important. I know some people are hung up on the baggage concept and all that … 'Oh, that's just the emotional baggage you carry from the past' or 'don't look back there, you're not going that way.'.

I always look back because my Ancestors lived back there, and I was taught not to turn away from where I came from – where I belong. I have learnt that many Aboriginal children were taken from their families, communities and culture, and so I should not take or keep anything for granted.

If RJS was part of the emotional freight I carried through life, then I am grateful for this sustaining emotional mass containing my mother's letters, feeding and growing my sense of belonging and love for being born into my family, clan, tribe and Nation. Our ancestors used the beautiful wooden thaga (coolamon) to carry precious loads such as water and babies, and I too carried precious articles in my thaga, the red RJS. I carried my memories in my thaga forward.

In 1978 I left hometown Mullewa on the bus, headed 600 km south for senior schooling in Perth with RJS holding my small-town possessions. Headed out of small rural living, a place where being a teenage mother was a top option and gossip prediction post-school: at least four girls claimed this achievement, white and Yamaji. I had my two sons over a decade after leaving Mullewa.

I lived for two years at an Aboriginal girls' hostel in Perth, we called it McKay Street, with RJS. I later found out the authorities called it Bentley House. We came from all over – Mullewa, Meekatharra, Mount Magnet, Wiluna, Onslow, Halls Creek and Broome. I currently work with one of the McKay Street hostel girls Wanda in Geraldton, our friendships have lasted the distance, and I met up with other hostel girls over the years in Wiluna, Nullagine, South

Hedland, Jigalong, Meekatharra, Adelaide and Geraldton. It was during my time at the hostel that Mum wrote me this series of letters from Mullewa. The same letters that were carefully packed away in RJS along with photographs, school reports and other notions I wanted to save for a rainy time … the same RJS letters that travelled with me to Mullewa, Canberra, Sydney, Brisbane, Geraldton, Perth and Port Hedland. I parted ways in the 1990s with RJS because the lock broke, and out to the South Hedland tip it went. I got a flasher suitcase to hold my values.

Oh, and Mum told me that after I was born at Eradu, I was taken to Geraldton where my first sleeping place was inside an old suitcase and then home to Four Corners in Mullewa with my suitcase.

… Papertalk is a Geraldton competitor's proposal, he says that the word was used years ago for sending a nigger from one camp to another—*Western Mail*, Perth, June 1928

Well, this Yamaji Nyarlu
is not your messenger
to lug colonial messages

Between your settlements
we carry our town
messages from our camps, right

Big around the globe
bet you didn't think that
possible 90 years ago

Paper talks everywhere now

We are our Ancestors
Descendants
Messengers

Nganajungu winja
Nganajungu gami
Gamigurdany
Nganajungu yagu
Yagugurdany
Nganajungu mama
Mamagurdany
Nganajungu aba
Abagurdany

Nganajungu winja Yamaji
Nganajungu winja nyarlu

Ngatha nganajungu yagu nganggurnmanha

                    I am still thinking about you my mother

Ngatha nganajungu mama nganggurnmanha

                    My father I am still thinking about you

Ngatha nganajungu gurda buwa nganggurnmanha

                    I am still thinking about you my old brother young brother

Ngatha nganajungu gantharri nganggurnmanha

                    My grandmother I think of you still

Ngatha nganajungu gami nganggurnmanha

                    I am still thinking about you my grandfather

Of the pages, their words bounce
off of me in the heart
slapping me awake 40 years on
ferrying dreams of better life
of parents only wanting best
I wanted different
away from and off a small town

Journey Beginning Things

Suitcase red girl teenager together
New space time moving thataway
Farewell waving family people mindset

Suitcase red a symbol of hopes
dreams and small-town big escape

Suitcase red carried years down
Reminder grounded family value
Possessions little clothes few

Suitcase red a symbol of bravery
adventure and expanding mind

Biliyarra thaga
Warlugura
Gagurlimanha
Biliyarra thaga

The teenage girl
leaving on her own
with her red coolamon

Messages

Spirit in the paper to be
carried miles across country to me
Mum should have been relaxing
before walking up to clean a public
space for money

Sipping a delicious
mug of tea
resting her body
before bending her knee
scrubbing floors, washing wards and clothes

Instead, she sat at an early morning table
before a family woke to letter write
on a late-night table when everyone's demands
stopped and went to sleep

To write these letters to me
I love these letters
still my family treasure

thana gagurlimanha:
separating from each other
moving apart away:
thana gagurlimanha
walgajunmanha:
writing letters
gaja barndimanmanha:
making daughter stronger
yagu barndimanmanha
making mother better:
murnamayimanha:
holding each other

Not Just Letters

These are not just letters on paper
these are mother's letters to me
her daughter, blood, her hopes
These are not letters on paper
that can be crumpled and discarded
a long line of forever flowing blood
of Yamaji women bound together
from a continuous womb of love

Bibarlu wangga paper talking
Bibarlu wangga because we can
Bibarlu wangga talking paper

They are not letters on paper
that can be burnt
Yagu's thoughts choose the words
Her mara wrote the sentences
despite leaving school at twelve
to be a servant slave kid to a society that despised her kind

Bibarlu wangga paper talking
Bibarlu wangga because we do
Bibarlu wangga talking paper

These are not letters on paper
that can be shredded
I close my eyes and see Yagu
this Yamaji woman
who would not allow her kids to starve
when money did, the times hard
but walk to the bush with a dog
and return with goat or marlu
slung over her shoulders to feed

Bibarlu wangga paper talking
Bibarlu wangga because we must
Bibarlu wangga talking paper

These are not just letters

Paper Love

Mum's love shown not often
-*nha*
Her
hugs
were
few
-*nha*
I did not blame Mum for that
Nanna
Alice
passed
away
young
-*nha*
Oh, but Mum's letters to me, that was
a different story, they are letters wrapped
-*manha*
in
love
in
way
that
I could feel the love hugs
-*manha*
springing
off
the
paper
-*manha*
Showing
a mother's
love
-*manha*

Mum's letters spoke to me

Paperbark

Paperbark bundle
wrapped stories
handed down
ceremony of time
to be etched in a mind
like a rock carving

Like a cave painting
paperbark bundle
wrapped
by Ancestor spirits

I don't know what
Wadjbellas call it
I don't see it in their world
but that's not important

Mum's letters speak to me

Letter on 28 June 1979

Dear Charmaine, sending cheque down for your glasses & when you pay for them tell them to send receipt to the box number you got I was very worried, so Mrs X wrote me a cheque out. By the time you get this I be ring you before. Love Mum

Nganajungu Yagu,

Thank you for sending me the money for new glasses and worrying about my eyesight. I did get shame when I became teenage four-eyes. I was supposed to wear my glasses for reading only back then, but now I wear them for driving and watching television. I wear them most times when there is no need, I have grown to like my glasses.

> It seems strange
> it really does
> to be wearing
> glasses

1.1

Foureyesfoureyesfoureyesfoureyesfoureyesfoureyesfoureyesfoureyes
Yalyba guru yalyba guru yalyba guru yalyba guru yalyba guru yalyba
Foureyesfoureyesfoureyesfoureyesfoureyesfoureyesfoureyesfoureyes
Yalybaguruyalybaguruyalybaguruyalybaguruyalybaguruyalybaguru

> Over the past forty years them glasses gurugilaaji ones
> helped me see so many things outside small little town
> opened my eyes they did as a teenager, mother, woman

1.2

Gurugilaajigurugilaajigurugilaajigurugilaajigurugilaajigurugilaajiguru
glasseseyeglasseseyeglasseseyeglasseseyeglasseseyeglasseseyeglasses
Gurugilaajigurugilaajigurugilaajigurugilaajigurugilaajigurugilaajiguru
glasseseyeglasseseyeglasseseyeglasseseyeglasseseyeglasseseyeglasses

> Yagu, they made me see and recognise the hardness
> life for Yamaji, family and mob right around Australia
> unfair treatment handed out by a colonial cruelty

1.3

migalgurnmanhamigalgurnmanhamigalgurnmanhamigalgurnmanha
emptyingoutemptyingoutemptyingoutemptyingoutemptyingoutempty
migalgurnmanhamigalgurnmanhamigalgurnmanhamigalgurnmanha
emptyingoutemptyingoutemptyingoutemptyingoutemptyingoutempty

> Yagu, gurugilaaji ones opened my eyes to a world angry towards
> people of colour – our people Yamaji - without good cause
> we are indeed body language experts, we can see things all
> They tried so hard to empty this land

1.4

Bajarnmanhabajarnmanhabajarnmanhabajarnmanhabajarnmanha
Beingangrybeingangrybeingangrybeingangrybeingangrybeing
Bajarnmanhabajarnmanhabajarnmanhabajarnmanhabajarnmanha
Beingangrybeingangrybeingangrybeingangrybeingangrybeing

> Yagu, I can see why our mob has been angry
> are angry, being angry, and still get it
> treatment of our mob in WA is a horror movie
> death in custody, in vans, in rivers, in health care services

1.5

barndijumanhabarndijumanhabarndijumanhabarndjimanhabarndijumanha
puttingitrightputtingitrightputtingitrightputtingitrightputtingitrightputting
barndijumanhabarndijumanhabarndijumanhabarndjimanhabarndijumanha
puttingitrightputtingitrightputtingitrightputtingitrightputtingitrightputting

> Yagu, I always remembered the beauty of our culture
> despite the racism seen in every step I took along years
> culture love was and is the anchor for everything done

Walgajunmanha All Time

We write about our existence pre-invasion / and that has made us visible
We write about our existence during invasion / and that keeps us visible

    walgajunmanha
        walgajunmanha
            walgajunmanha

We write about the blood they spilt / and that honours ancestors' memories
We write about the land they stole / and that shows they are savage thieves

            walgajunmanha
        walgajunmanha
    walgajunmanha

We write about our connection to country / and that challenges theirs
We write about our lived realities / and that shows them we survived

    walgajunmanha
        walgajunmanha
            walgajunmanha

We write about sky world knowledge / and show them the first astronomers
We write about earth world knowledge / and show them a sustainable culture

            walgajunmanha
        walgajunmanha
    walgajunmanha

We write about traditional food production / and contest their agriculture
We write about traditional mud huts / and debunk their walkabout romanticism

    walgajunmanha
        walgajunmanha
            walgajunmanha

We write about Aboriginal deaths in custody / and show them we fight back
We write about deaths in police presence / and we are not blinded by lies

            walgajunmanha
        walgajunmanha
    walgajunmanha

We write about racism experiences / punctures in their ethnocentric balloons
We write about campaign for Aboriginal rights / pens our weapon of choice

    walgajunmanha
        walgajunmanha
            walgajunmanha

We write about deep Aboriginal culture love /
            and that shatters their assimilation into pieces

Letter on 6 April 1978

Darling Toots, received your always loving letter today. Forgive me for not writing sooner you know how much I hate writing it's not I haven't forgotten you. I think of you always and worry about you but darling I know you can look after yourself as you always said ... your forever loving mother Margaret x

Nganajungu Yagu

I stumbled through teenage years
of hope dreams, drunkenness
clutching a small parcel of letters
Letters from home and belonging
through those dangerous times
When life's path entertains many tracks
Thank our Ancestors for there are many
crossroads if you recognise
I pushed on through motherhood
baby cargo nothing else mattered
Those letters now tucked away safe
in my red suitcase cave
for another time and moment away
Your phone call satisfied with words
when Ancestors called to take you
nothing I could do for this is the way
I longed to hear your voice
For you were now the one to leave me
visiting me in dreams to soothe
Your letters a mark of existence and
your energy bursting off its pages

Thank you for doing what you hated
and I celebrate

widara bariya: long track
widara ruudu: long road

Cheque School Kids

We all received
three-dollar cheque
then we gottem six-dollar

Yamaji kids that is
high school incentive

every fortnight to deposit
in bankbook
or cash at shop
we had to nurse cause

no rich families us
we could buy:

>   stamps, tampons, lollies
>   ice creams and bus fares

into Perth city to check
out the mob

Bibarlu
Marda
Marn.gurr
Yamaji nyarlu

Gutharra 2: More Than a Yarn

Darling Toots, good to know that you are happy down there. It pleases Dad and myself to know that you are happy. Every time Dad reads the letters you write It brings tears to his eyes … Your forever loving mother Margaret x

Nganajungu Yagu,

I have seen Dad's tears before but not the tears you write about – tears for his teenage daughter's achievements. This was very special, Mum, thank you for telling me – I carried this knowledge to give me strength moving forward in life. I remember asking Dad about 35 years ago why he was drunk, crying, and he just said, 'You wouldn't understand.' This made me even more curious about his childhood, and I asked myself questions like – Why did he distance himself from his family? Why he was an angry man? Why did I feel a sadness from within him? Why did he drink so much and then become violent? I needed to understand more about Dad's upbringing and childhood because he was also good and kind. In the past 20 years I have been reading Dad's Native Welfare records, and he was institutionalised by his family quite young. At the age of six years old he was placed in New Norcia Mission, 300 km south of where his family lived. Not many people talk about the kids that were placed in New Norcia Mission by their families, do they? You know, the ones that were not Stolen Generation, but robbed of their childhood outside of an institution. When I lived in South Hedland, I met a cousin of Dad's who told me of the time they tried to escape but got caught. Part of their punishment was to have their heads shaved and to wear a chaff bag. I am not sure if this escape was from New Norcia or Moore River Native Settlement. When we lived in Mullewa next to Our Lady of Mount Carmel church, the nuns offered to give me piano lessons, but Dad went off his head and said 'no' when I asked him. I reckon he suffered the same cruelty in the kids' prison at the hands of the New Norcia religious assholes as did all the other 'inmates' – this is what they were called, nyorn. He would have been treated the same – just another fair Aboriginal boy, an 'inmate', in a sick colonial Western Australian system with social engineering experiments under the guise of the *Aboriginal Act* 1905. When Dad was around 15 years old, he was sent to Moore River Native Settlement for an 'indefinite' period for receiving stolen goods in the form of some cash from another teenager.

Two older sisters recently shared a story Dad told them:

Dad waited until it rained and took off from Moore River on foot home to Coodingnow Station. He made it home and on his return his Grandfather Clinch sent him to an outcamp to look after camels and horses on his own. He had his own horse and would ride across the Badimaya country, sometimes sneaking back to the station. When the authorities went to Coodingnow to look for Dad they could not find him. Dad said this was the most loneliness time of his life living at the outcamp but when he returned to Coodingnow he was older and was a free man. Dad headed to Perth for a little while before returning to Paynes Find Mount Magnet area.

I believe the childhood trauma Dad faced in these institutions came down through generations, this is what I have come to understand. I write now and shed tears for Dad, that little boy locked away creating a sadness that flowed on to to me, his daughter, other family members, the next generations. Intergenerational trauma is real, and moves through generations if we don't recognise it and deal. I write now and shed tears for the many children who never ever made it back.

Yagu, when I read Dad's Native Welfare files, I shed many tears as part of understanding his, and work towards healing and telling his story to family – children, grand- and great-. Yet, despite this part of his childhood, Dad always told us he was a proud Badimaya man and proud of his connection to his maternal grandmother's Badimaya culture and country. Nyorn, where was his RJS? Did it exist for him? Could it exist for him? Was he stripped of everything?

> Crying out for his mother
> *Bibi: Bibi: Bibi: Bibi: Bibi: Bibi*
> from within the cold confines
> of damp children prison camps
> carrying out the dirty work
> religious group wanting child slaves

Crying out for his grandmother
Gami: Gami: Gami: Gami: Gami: Gami
to comfort her Gami-grandson locked inside
away from his little brothers
Locked away hundreds and miles from home

Did Gami see Gami again?

Gurriya: uno: one
Gudha: dos: two
Gadyardi: tres: three
Gudha-gudhara: cuatro: four
Mara Gurriya: cinco: five

Us kids laughed when
Dad counted in Spanish

We didn't know
what this meant
where he learnt this

We had no idea
Dad laughed with us
but sometimes he cried

Now every time
I think about New Norcia
and Dad being inside
I cry for him that child

Balu wangga Spanish
Balu wangga Badimaya
Balu wangga English

I see: I seen
I feel: I felt
I hear: I heard
I learn: I learnt

Family together		Racism
Ancestral teachings		Sexism
Elder respect		Elder abuse
Love for land		Cultural genocide
Customs intact		Assimilation
Beliefs intact		Child trauma
Kangaroo shooting		Grog abuse
Collecting emu eggs		Domestic violence
Bush food knowledge		Family violence
Sand into water		Community violence
Dancing culture	**I**	Police brutality
Language use	**Understand**	Racial profiling
Death customs	**I**	Colonisation
Decolonisaton	**Know**	Meth takeover
Painting stories		Drug abuse
Singing stories		Sexual abuse
Boomerang music		Industry racism
Bimba bush lolly		Land theft
Wattle seed damper		Native title corruption
Grinding stones		Grief fatigue
Smoking ceremonies		Archive grief
Bush medicine		Paper genocide
Diversity respect		Death in custody
Writing our stories		Housing racism

Birthday Present

A first birthday present
from Mum and Dad
big and leather-bound
a Holy Bible printed 1957
authorised King James Version
I don't know what that means?

The first page reads:
> *Presented to Charmaine Joy*
> *By Mum & Dad*
> *Date 29-1-1963*
> *Happy Birthday Age 1 year*

I still have what is left
that Bible with half
pages missing out of its 1300
The pages with the paintings
remain I only kept this book because a gift

My faith is in our Ancestors
their teachings, words, spirituality
I can't believe in these
other alien cults
responsible for so much
damage with lies, cultural genocide, abuse

My younger brother said:
> *I remember that Bible*
> *I liked to look at the pictures*
> *inside from some painters*
> *like Michelangelo types*

We all liked to look
the paintings from a world
removed in distance
and in time from us in Mullewa
Raphael, Rembrandt, Giulio Romano
Jean Baptiste-Camille Corot, Andrea Vaccaro

I hadn't looked at this Bible
for over 20 years and today
I stare at those paintings again
and began to think about
why my parents gifted this to me

I wondered was it because
little baby sister Camelia
passed away when Mum
was three months pregnant
and I was born six months later?

Letter on 6 April 1978

Darling Toots, with me working again has been a godsend to us at home no more worries about food the kids are not wanting for anything like before … Your forever loving mother Margaret

Each letter spoke of food
The need for food spoke
through each letter

Gulydyirrabaya

Mother's food worries never seemed
to end when eating dry Weetbix
butter or vegemite is all

Gulydyirrabaya

When food was scarce
when food was plentiful
the words flowed like a pot
stew bubbling on

Gulydyirrabaya

To feed the family
no one was hungry
no one was going to starve
The bookups will be paid
The family and friends
food cadging can rest

Gulydyirrabaya

There will be no more
worries about food
when work is here

Gulydyirrabaya

Marn.gurr 3: More Than a Yarn: House Dreams

Darling Toots, received your always loving letter today … we are first getting on our feet again only one big problem is catching up on rent but things will come good since I started work … Your forever loving mother Margaret xxx

Nganajungu Yagu,

I need to tell you about this memory and the impact it had on me, the one when you and Dad did not catch up on the rent, and you had forgotten to tell me that you got evicted. I caught the Westrail bus home from Perth for school holidays, bus driver even dropped me at the front of 67 Maitland Road. I knocked on the door, looked through the window, the house was empty. I had no idea where my family had gone to in Mullewa. I know it was a small town, but the shock of going home to a house that would never be my home again was hard. I vowed then, as a 17-year-old, never to rent state government owned social housing, and I never have. I have lived in Aboriginal hostels, friends' homes, university residentials, private rentals, but steered away from social housing. I did find you all at a private rental on Dalgety Street – never did like that house, though, because it was just too close to the Club Hotel. One of my first university essays was called 'white racism', about how housing was used to put the racist assimilation policy into practice.

I created a map showing the housing movement of Yamajis from Mullewa Reserve to Four Corners, then the Maley Street and Dalgety Street areas. I was in my mid-20s when I became a first-home buyer in South Hedland on Greene Place. It wasn't the flashiest house, but it sure was better than being controlled by some government department, and now being mortgage-free later in life is a good position to be in. I would have to say that becoming a home owner is one of the best decisions made in my young life. This decision had nothing to do with the Wadjbella's way of living or an assimilation into white Australia. No, I really didn't like what happened back then, Mum, with the eviction, and how the family suffered in those times at the mouth of the state government. In hindsight, my experience of the eviction has helped me stay upright throughout my life, and I am glad you got to stay with me in South Hedland and then in Utakarra, Geraldton. The little ramp made for your wheelchair at the Utakarra house is still outside, nyorn.

Government social housing
matchstick house living
smashed at any moment
by the fists of authorities

I often think of Dad's housing stories, and how hard he tried to provide shelter for us children. He had dreams of building his own house in Mount Magnet, then in Mullewa. The older sisters have shown me the concrete pad Dad laid down on the Mount Magnet reserve to build a house for them. That dream didn't go past the concrete pad, still baking there now in the sun. I don't know much more of that housing dream. Then, later, in Mullewa, Dad purchased a vacant block of land on Dalgety Street. Jenny said we were all excited about this block and would often run down to check it out – maybe we just stood in the space and dreamed about the house that would be ours. I remember the block, a barren piece of land that became slippery when it rained, and it still is. I still drive past that block and stare at it when I visit Mullewa. I think us kids were proud that Dad had purchased it and it belonged to him. That housing dream got crushed when the Native Welfare Board would not support Dad with a loan to build a modest three-bedroom house on the block for his family. Dad gave up chasing his housing dreams after that and settled into the social housing merry-go-round. He didn't pay the rates, and the shire took it. Now, reflecting, maybe all these family housing dreams and experiences contributed to my dislike of government. I feel sad that Dad's dreams did not become. I did carry his dreams in my RJS across the years.

Badimaya bagali
your gulu dreams
did not disappear
we carried it forward

30% of Aboriginal people
own homes in Geraldton
and I am one of them.

Letter on 6 April 1978

Darling Toots ... I have to work tomorrow and that's more important to me than drink. I have experienced all the hardship without work, you kids are more important to me. I said to Dad all I am going to live for now is the kids. I am sick of being without money ... Your forever loving mother Margaret xx

Nganajungu Yagu,

I agree there is a lot of hardship without work. I see it all around me and growing up with that hardship certainly helped me understand that money is needed to live in this world we now wake in. I watched you and Dad struggle, but still go on working when it was available. You would walk up to the Mullewa hospital in your green uniform and do the job of a domestic – cleaning wards, mopping and polishing floors, loading the washing machines and ironing the clothes. Dad's seasonal jobs as a shearer, then sandalwood contractor, were equally hard. We all got excited to see the money that came from hard work. It wasn't a lot of money, but enough to meet our need.

I like working and have done so since I was 17 years of age. I had time off to have my sons, of course, but then, with the support of relatives and childcare centres, went straight back into the workforce. One of my sisters says I am a workaholic – I think she might be right – but it's something I don't regret. The opportunities and experiences from working outweighed not working, that's for sure. I always remember the hardship of our Ancestors and Elders working as slaves on Western Australian stations, farms and in towns. The Western Australian government made sure a slavery system existed – employers required government-approved permits to employ our people. Aboriginal wages went into government buckets disguised as Aboriginal welfare funds. I know you became part of this slavery system from a very young age, and I am grateful for all your hard work and challenges. The assimilation policy and slavery systems held hands in Western Australia, this we all need to remember. Our people were and remain hardworking.

Tea Leaves Stains

Café sitting teacup drinking
Tea leaves tell a story

You know slavery

Poured through generation eyes
swirling into existence
with each teaspoon stir
stirring memories not forget
Wadjbellas took something

Society slavery here

Like domesticating a cat or breaking
a wild horse the gin needs to serve us
that's their lot was the
catchcry of the day

mission slavery real

A fine cup saucer lace
for the mijiji white woman
fancy embroidered tablecloth
stained enamel mug chipped
for the nyarlu black woman
station domestics locked in

station slavery existed

Our mothers the tea tray girls
serving cakes, tea and coffee
white uniform in white spaces
station house or town tearooms
but not their space to domesticate

Domestics were slaves

Wanggamanha: Talking: Listening: Nganggurnmanha

Summer nights still and warm by still
dimensions of mattresses dragged outside
cyclone beds added moved into place
car bonnets came in handy

> *Wanggamanha: talking*
> *Wanggajimanha: all talking together*

Escaping heat trapped heat in
fibro and tin rented homes
social housing stingy government
means no insulation for renters

> *Ngarlbungga: the hot season*
> *Wanggajimanha: all talking together*

In this cover darkness cover the
storytellers would emerge
we would scream, cry
laugh, reflect, be silenced
fight for storytelling rights

> *Ngardunggayimanha: getting dark night-time*
> *Wanggajimanha: all talking together*

The older ones would make us
scream with the tap
kangaroo claw on tin
stones thrown on the roof
calming back with hard laughs

> *Ngurlumanmanha: scaring us*
> *Wanggajimanha: all talking together*

Our Oldies would make us sad talking
about family who had gone
on to join our Ancestors ahead
keeping their memory alive

Nganggunmanha: remembering
Wanggajimanha: all talking together

We would be made to belly laugh
From funny or silly things, we
saw or did during the week
body actions and all with it

Jurnimanha: laughing
Wanggajimanha: all talking together

Our many matriarchs made us
understand importance
when looking up into great
Milky Way across wide night sky
width offering precious gifts of
cultural teachings transfer on

Miyarnuwimanha: learning
Wanggajimanha: all talking together

Emu egg season linked to
Emu in the sky linked to
Teaching how to track back to
Teaching methods linked to
Yamaji Ancestors long before

Jirdilungu: Milky Way
Wanggajimanha: all talking together

Other times we would simply count
Count the many satellites orbiting
the Earth seeing the light moving
across the night sky disappearing
arguing over who saw the most

> *Murdiyimanha: becoming cold winter*
> *Wanggajimanha: all talking together*

On the cooler winter nights a warm
fire lured a circle
around its flames' light warmth
not wanting to miss a word
or a yarn, a story or a teaching to carry
Carry into adulthood to pass on

Soothing into a dreamlike state

> *Wanggajimanha: all talking together*
> *Wanggamanha: talking*

Dust at Dusk

Afternoon sea breeze sometimes
carries mother's gentle whispering
reminding don't forget the ways
in lattes and Facebook distractions before dusk
bush broom this awaits a yard
Ancestors echo through time

> *Dust at dusk and stones flying*
> *ground sweeping for a healthy mind*

A woman's daily dance for good
spirits move within the memory ground
Bush broom stirs dust and land
keeping a family from hands
in the shadows of opportunity

> *Dust at dusk and stones flying*
> *Spiritual ritual resisting town life*

The bush broom gone in time
Colonisation has not disrupted the night
thoughts of yard movements
matriarchal teaching and healing
eases through our generation's veins
keeping watch on mobs of family tree

Bushbroom

balygurr yagu
balygurr maraji
balygurr gantharri

balygurr jundanmanha
      jundanmanha
      jundanmanha
      jundanmanha
      jundanmanha

jundanmanha mungaly-mungaly
          mungaly-mungaly
          mungaly-mungaly
          mungaly-mungaly
          mungaly-mungaly
          mungaly-mungaly

balygurr jirrararda
      jirrararda
      jirrararda
      jirrararda
      jirrararda
      jirrararda

balygurr yagu
balygurr maraji
balygurr gantharri

Letter on 26 October 1979

Dear Charmaine, at last I got around to writing to you its that long since I've written a letter. I don't know how to write properly. All the kids are well at home only Dad is down with the flu … your loving Mother always xx

Nganajungu Yagu,

I don't think the kids are well anymore. Today your grandson said this:

> *I miss Nan Margaret I always think of her and*
> *what it would have been like if she was here.*
> *I would have been with her right now in Mully*

Yagu,
I don't think the kids are coping here now.
I feel like I must tread so lightly like.
Walking on eggs around some.

Yagu,
I don't think the kids are well anymore.

You worried about all children in your family – grandchildren, great-grandchildren, nieces and nephews. There was no nuclear family by your eyes, your ways. Beautiful trait. But, oh, a burden – carrying that sometimes heavy tree. I know your favourite saying was 'they are my people', and how you would give your daily last in so saying. I understand feeling, that responsibility, obligation and burden more now since you left us.

> Sat at court hearings / police cell welfare checks / prison visits / family lawyer talks / responsible person for underage family lock-ups / magistrates / argued with cops / bus fares for domestic violence victims / brought food so young family could eat / suicide-watched young family / organised mental care for family / organised accommodation / organised funerals / seen busted faces of violence / seen family breakdown from substance / advocated on housing / seen effects of meth / cleaned houses after evictions / moved furniture / lent money that never came back / family

Yagu,

You did this and more.

I crouch in your shadow of awesomeness.

I coped only with your strong spirit behind me, supporting and giving, a strength to deal anything to life playing me.

Many family members are well, and getting on, but there are members who aren't.

Yagu,

I don't think the kids are well anymore, and it hurts.

It is hurtful.

Where does their pain go to when they don't use help around them or the trust leaves?

Gurninyimanha mayu
Mayu bajayimanha
Warritharrayimanha mayu
Mayu ngarlayigayimanha
Gudurdu warritharra
Gudurdu warritharra
Gudurdu warritharra

Letter on 26 October 1979

Dear Charmaine … All the Papertalks are well also Collards and Comeagains, except Aunty X she is in hospital in Geraldton with a fractured leg … well I might close now I have to do a bit of work before I go off to work and don't forget to write back soon and lots of love to you and look after yourself … Your loving Mother always xxxxxxxxx

Nganajungu Yagu,

One of the things I loved about your letters was the news and stories about family, not just immediate, but all. I loved hearing about the babies being born, the family visiting Mullewa, aunties', brothers' and sisters' movements, and even the fights up the Club Hotel. The closeness you had with your brother, sisters and their families. I haven't seen that type of connection since all you oldies left us here – things, different now – we all meet up at funerals now, mostly. I have to say the native title process contributed to some family tree dropped branches, but I think it was all the Elders passing. They were the bond keeping the extended trunk strong. I am hoping it doesn't take our clan too many generations to recover.

I learnt from you that being grounded includes strong connection. I know the branches on your side, but not to the same level on Dad's. I am learning as I grow, writing everything down. I write this because coming from an oral tradition society has been disastrous in the handing down of knowledge about our old people, Ancestors, in this now. Yagu, the oral history you have handed down about family is invaluable. I believe and stick by everything you handed down but, by gee, some anthropologists have white ethnocentric lenses. If Ancestors didn't come in contact with the Whiteman through police records, 'chief protector of Aborigines' records, 'native' welfare records, station owners, Daisy Bates records or Tindale records, then Aboriginal oral history is not seen as legitimate. I cannot accept how Yamaji family oral history is undervalued in Australia. This is traumatising for many Aboriginal people, families on traditional country.

Anyways, I have been reading your Colonial records – aka Native Welfare files – and I read how in the 1950s you had applied for the infamous Western Australia Native Citizenship Rights. I am not sure how this process made life easier for your family.

You still lived in Aboriginal housing.
You still had records to monitor your life.
You still had to go into the blacks-only bar.
You still lived in the Aboriginal town areas.
You still had a 'native' reserve on outskirts.
You still weren't welcome at the movies.
And the list goes.

It looked like a racist bullshit process to be part of a White Australian society when you belonged to the first peoples of the land. Australian apartheid policy, in practice, is what this all was. Australia must own what it did, write it into its history since Colonisation – invasion – settlement by colonial boat immigrants.

What I want to say to you is how glad I am that you didn't stick to the colonial cultural genocide requirements of Form 2. Assimilation has not been and isn't good for Yamaji – trying to make everyone white by acting white but not being white. A dangerous space. Who makes their way better than anyone else? Nothing unna! Nobody.

Cultural Genocide

1.1

```
Western Australian Natives (Citizenship Rights) Regulation Form 2
```

Question 7: Has the Applicant **DISSOLVED** tribal and native association for two years except for respect to lineal descendant or native relations of the first degree?

My answer:

> They put on the hat, the glove and
> dress to please you, but to terminate
> and split up with family, no, that wasn't
> going to happen for many. They just
> said yes to get the certificate, that's
> all. Some might have gone the whole
> way to break up with their relatives,
> but they came back through their
> children and descendants. I see them
> sitting at native title meetings, visiting
> country, searching for connection.
> No dissolving and disappearing for
> everyone.

1.2

Question 8: Has the Applicant adopted the manner and habits of **CIVILISED LIFE**? If so, for how long to your knowledge?

My answer:

> We have lived a civilised life for over 60,000 years on a land with advanced fire-stick farming, traditional knowledge, no ocean plastic floating islands, abundance of foods without plastic wrappings, foot energy, no fuel pollution, seasonal harvesting on land without heavy fertilisers to poison rivers.

1.3

Western Australian Natives (Citizenship Rights) Regulation Form 2

Question 9: Does the Applicant live according to **WHITE** standards?

My answer:

> I am not sure what white standards
> are, but our women have cleaned your
> homes, raised your children, nursed
> your babies. Our men cleared our
> lands for your crops, showed you our
> fresh waterholes, showed you our land,
> offered you yams and bush foods. All
> according to our standards. Our people
> made sure you could survive on our
> land.

1.4

Question 10: Does the Applicant or his wife **CONSORT** with natives?

My answer:

We consort with our people. All the
time, and that never stopped. We have
lookouts to tell if you are coming into
our space, to fool you. Our families are
our greatest treasures, did you think
we would abandon them because you
said so? A lot of you consorted with us,
that's why you took our children away
… to hide your shame.

1.5

Western Australian Natives (Citizenship Rights) Regulation Form 2

Question 11: Does the Applicant or his wife visit the camps of **NATIVE RELATIONS** or do relatives visit them?

My answer:

> Our mob played cards together – big gambling school camps on hills in Mullewa. They had singsongs (you might call them corroboree) on the Reserve, up the Common and other places. They had to visit each other, cultural obligations. Where do you think people went when kicked out of town at 6 p.m. curfew? What do you think happened at Murgoo Races, Landor Races? Not only horse racing for the Yamaji attending – singsong and socialising.

DISSOLVED

CIVILISED LIFE

WHITE

CONSORT

NATIVE RELATIONS

CITIZENSHIP

OF WHAT

Letter on 1 November 1979

Dear Charmaine, just writing a short note to say we are ok, sorry I didn't write sooner. I seem to be on the move all the time feeling tired and weary … doctor told me he saw you in a café he was quite thrilled he told me twice … I am writing this in a hurry … its 6.30 Friday morning and have to be at work 7am. Sending five dollars will send more later had to pay all bills, will close now love from us all at home. Thinking of you always. From your loving Mother x

Nganajungu Yagu,

I totally loved the short notes and letters, it was this contact between us that gave me the boost to remain on track … I don't think I really understood that until now … I added all your letters and notes to my thaga RJS to empower me … carried like the water of life. I love that I can read your letters and look at your handwriting and think to myself 'my mum wrote that'. I am sitting here, sipping my cup of tea, thinking about all that work you had to do to survive. You started so young, so yes I understand your tiredness. A lot of the younger generation doesn't know that type of hard work or the sacrifices your generation made. Life was tough, hey? I totally appreciate everything you did for all us. I now know that things back home were tougher than you let on. Last year I saw some files documenting your stress and health condition back then … at that time I felt sad and regretful that I had to leave Mullewa, but I was just a kid trying to find my way in the big world … and I know you pushed me towards a better life. That life took a long time coming but it is kinda here now … I am in my mid-50s, and my life is okay for me … I need to say, Mum, that for many years I carried guilt about leaving my younger siblings, like I had deserted them. And in recent years, a couple of them have said they felt that I did desert and abandon them. That was hard to take. Resentment towards me is not something of my making, nor of theirs. It has taken many years to resolve these feelings, and I am still working on the impact of leaving my younger siblings. Siblings fight, but in our hearts there is no hate … only family love.

I remember seeing Doctor in a Barrack Street café in Perth on the weekend when I was in CBD, strolling about as teenage girls do. Our meeting was a pleasant surprise for both of us, and we had a good old yarn. He was a good doctor and had a way with the Yamaji community … I don't know what the doctors are like in Mullewa now, but you will be sad to know the old hospital is being demolished for some new health service building. There are mixed feelings in the community, understandable with all the memories of births, deaths, working ladies and, of course, your last home after you had the stroke. I know I will be sad when it's demolished. Many changes from your days ... even though there is no 'meat safe' ward for Yamaji only at the back of the hospital ... the memories still remain with some of us.

Thaga RJS
carried like
water of life
sustaining the
spiritual and
cultural needs
and protection
like a young mother
carrying her baby
in the thaga on country

Family Food List

Kangaroo tail brawn
Marlu nyurndi
Stuffed eggplant
Pig's head, baked
Nani maga gambu
Kangaroo, fry-up
Marlu guga gambu
Damper fluffy
Dambamanmanha
Ice cream, homemade
Sheep tripe
Jiibu warri
Sheep runners
Jiibu nyurililiny
Kangaroo, stew
Marlu gambu
Rhubarb and custard
Lamb tails, grilled
Jiibu nyurndi
Weetbix, dry
Weetbix and milk
Goanna, sand goanna
Guwiyarl guga gambu
Rice and milk
Sheep's head, baked
Jiibu maga gambu
Liver, fried

Jiibu bitharn
Sweetbread, fried
Jiibu thalba
Quondongs, raw
Warlgu fruit
Sandalwood nuts
Warlarda
Polony tomato sauce
Corned beef, tinned
Marrow, stuffed
Flaps, grill-up
Jiibu bimbily
Bread and butter
Edible witchetty grub
Bardi's, sometimes
Tree gum
Bimba, seasonal
Bush onion
Ngarlgu
Pea and ham soup
Goat, baked
Nani gambu
Goat, stew
Nani gambu
Irish stew, tinned
Emu egg, scrambled
Yalibirri warla

Letter on 1 November 1979

*Dear Charmaine, received your letter yesterday and was pleased to hear from you ... **I know that you have** **done well at school** keep up the good work ... only wish I was there to see you, but I am always with you in my thoughts... can picture your ways. I never had the education ... I hope things work out for you darling 'Toots' Charmaine ... love Mum and Dad.*

Nganajungu Yagu,

I have learnt that we don't lose ourselves or our cultural connections when we get educated in the Whiteman's system or, as the educated say, the Western system. I was an average student, and my biggest strength was the courage to stay engaged in schooling for the twelve years. I know a lot of Yamaji kids that didn't stay for one reason or another. I love the story my six older siblings share about taking me to Sandstone School with them. They said I was pushed in the pram to school and sat in the classroom corner watching them. My oldest brother would be naughty and skid around with me in the pram hanging on, red dust flying. Anyways, my journey into the classroom started when I was around two years old, so maybe that had something to do with me liking the school environment. I don't know. What I do know is that I didn't see many options for young Yamaji girls other than being teenage mothers. I experienced enough teenage gendered violence to want something different in life, and I felt education and the school offered something elsewhere. That's what family, teachers and others told me, and I believed them. Yagu, my first day in the city school was just terrifying, hundreds of students. I ended up in the bathrooms hiding and crying because I was too ashamed to ask anyone for directions. I wanted to come home, but didn't want to disappoint you and Dad. I didn't want to disappoint myself. I love the support you gave, Yagu, through your phone calls and letters ... the support of being with all the other country Aboriginal girls in Bentley House on McKay Street. The support of family living in Perth, we always went across to Redcliffe for visits and to hang. I made a couple of good friends at school – enough to survive for the two years there. Cousin Katie was there for one year at the same time as me before heading up to South Hedland. That made a big difference, our cousin sister friendship has lasted. She finished Year 12 and I finished Year 12, so I think we both did good. I am keeping up the good work, still studying, but this time doing a scary PhD, the first but not the last in our family. I am undertaking an autoethnography, and writing about moments of my life that made a change, it's very challenging, exciting and hard work. I am sure you and Dad would have been proud. I will come for a visit to the Mullewa cemetery and tell you both all about this next journey.

I wrote the following in my 1979 school journal (which I have still have and like a bower bird, I keep things).

Monday 26 Nov 1979

Dear Journal,

Schools well and truly over now and I may never see any of the kids again. But as I keep telling myself life must go on and all good things must come to an end. I guess I'm scared. School life is all I've known and now it has come to an end and I have to step into another world. Destiny Unknown.

> *School,*
> *I must*
> *say goodbye*
> *No!*
> *I won't cry*
> *I'm going*
> *to be*
> *Brave and strong*
> *I'm going*
> *to step out*
> *Into that*
> *waiting world*
> *School,*
> *I will*
> *remember you*
> *Good-Bye!*

Letter on 1 November 1979

Dear Charmaine … I am proud of you it uplifts me when I am down and worried it gives me strength to carry on working to know that I have something to work for … love from all at home … Love Mum and Dad.

Nganajungu Yagu,

> My heart bursts
> on pride
> thinking about you
> worked so
> hard mopping
> floors laundry sweating
> home worries
> you carried and carried

I am trying to let you know how proud of you I am, your words gave me strength and inspiration to move ahead as a teenager into the wide white world. Just like when you wrote that I as a teenager gave you strength. I now know life was extremely hard for you as a woman and a mother back home, when all I wanted was to go and explore a world beyond what I knew. I have come to understand a lot about you, Yagu, through your early-year teachings, the stories shared and now the files I read about you and your life. The challenges you faced as a pre-teen, having your mother pass away, you had to grow up fast and fend. Your first job was being a tray maid at the Mullewa hospital. There was a group photo including a teenage you on the hospital wall. I don't know where that framed photo has disappeared to. I asked at the Mullewa hospital last year where the photo is now, nobody seems to know. Wish I had a copy. Mum, you knew the meaning of hard work from an early age, and you taught me well about ethics. I know that you were proud of all your kids because in one of your letters you wrote:

> *… I never had the education but you, Charlie and Alex made up for that, proud of that for that proud of you all … never let Mum down but the others made it up in other ways …*

Sadness and grief surrounded you. I know you never spoke of your babies passing, but you did make sure we knew of their burial sites in the Mullewa cemetery, and I, in turn, have passed this information on to younger family members. I continue to make sure memory of their existence remains – they are our brothers and sisters. They are your children. I often think of what it would have been like if they had survived and were here with us, especially the twin brothers ten months younger than me. Then, when you lost your eldest son … well, that was the hardest thing for me to ever do, giving you that sad news, and I don't believe you ever recovered from that sadness. I don't know how to understand this type of trauma. I don't even understand how you survived losing five babies in a seven-year period. Yagu, you were a strong and courageous woman, and it is me who is so proud of you, all the struggles and challenges you endured over your 73 years. I now understand why you and Dad gave me a Bible for my first birthday. A present never carried in RJS. I don't remember how it found its way back to me. Yagu, maybe it was in your box when you passed or I picked it out of possessions when relocating you back to Mullewa?

Wall

1961 Camelia Rosemary: Row D Plot B #5

1962 Peter & John: Row D Plot B #7

1965 Jeannie Marie: Row A Plot C #8

1968 Stillborn: burial unknown

Yalyba 4: More Than a Yarn

Nganajungu Yagu,

I have your colonial records – referred to mostly as 'Native Welfare files'. They are not easy to read, but I feel necessary to read. This is the Western Australian government's legacy, cruel and race-based systems that enforced cultural genocide. Yagu, I don't know if you ever saw your file? Maybe it wasn't a done thing back then to ask for your personal government files? I have family files. One of the things that gripped my attention was the stamping of all the file notes – I have photographed the three most prominent.

Can you see this book? Are you reading over my shoulder?

The government energy used to try and stamp Yamaji into the ground … hey, we survived to read them. I have heard yarns that when the Department of Native Welfare (DNW), Geraldton Branch, closed, most files there were destroyed. It is said departmental records and files were placed in a heap and burnt. I believe this possible, with the abrupt closure of ATSIC Geraldton, a skip bin was brought in to dispose of 'things'. I was there at the time. I also heard that some of the DNW employees took files and documents and still have them. I don't know how I feel about this, especially if they are reading files not belonging to them or their families. I thank them for salvaging documents and records, but if these yarns are true, they must hand records back to some safekeeping place for the other families to access and own. Data sovereignty means we should possess, access and own our data, and this includes 'native welfare files'.

...

...

...

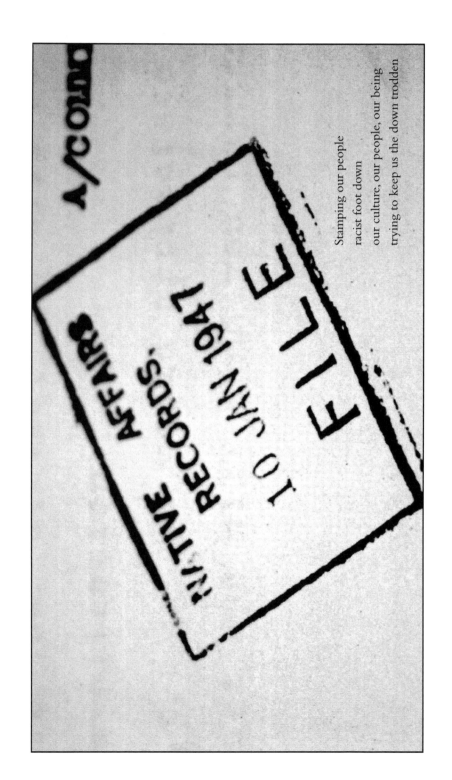

Stamping our people
racist foot down
our culture, our people, our being
trying to keep us the down trodden

Stamp Yamaji out
stamp out a race
first people get
stamping in Assimilation

Stamp Yamaji
blood into soil
biological warfare terrorism
breeding out the black
when culture isn't skin

Buried Deep

Buried
within

Womb
mother,
Earth

Warm
protected
flows

Powerful
energy
in and is me

We Can, We Do, We Will!

We can stand at our ground because of her
a silhouette symbol of beautiful resistance resilience
Shells wrapped regally around her neck
eyes looking deep into the generations
A reminder of woman's strength drawn from long lines
from a long line of female Ancestors

> *Truganinni elegant stance of survival and*
> *remembrance for there will be no forgetting*
> *or erasure of such strength and existence*

We can raise our voices because of her
like a slap sudden clap of thunder shooting
between the earth world and sky world
Demanding visibility, presence and words
lifting the veil of oppression to reveal
voices from Earth mother and her womb's raging

> *Oodgeroo Noonuccal pen was a bush broom*
> *Willy-willy sweeping words and energy across*
> *Country preparing for literature warriors to come*

Because of her we can maintain our faith in hope
creating a just and better society for our peoples
Fighting for Indigenous rights and setting the path
for 1967 Referendum with a gentle smile
A fire in the belly beacon against injustices

> *Faith Bandler showed us people power*
> *can turn a country's vote into an affirmative*
> *Activism can work towards social change*

Long line women many energies
holding Indigenous women's universe
Powers, strengths, struggles, fights and wins
Maternal Ancestors, family and friends
at the camp site, kitchen and meeting room.
A gallery, a stage, a sports field, a studio, a home

> *Holding us tight and holding us*
> *up so we can hold our families and tackle hurdles*
> *We don't give up and it is because they didn't*

Nurture

Nurture me
protect
me

watch me grow
Nobody can
stop me

It is strong
for my
Ancestors
are behind me
and
in front of me

I remain
Gaja
I remain
Mayu
Thaga wrapped

Letter on 1 November 1979

Dear Charmaine … I am proud of you that's why I am sitting here crying letting it all out … ring MW 9 and ask for me to ring you. Can tell you more news but excited about you … its beautiful something to experience, don't be afraid of the big Jet, have courage my mind is with you, first time on plane … love you always mother … Love Mum and Dad xxx

Nganajungu Yagu,

It's been over 39 years since I boarded that first flight east to Canberra, and I don't remember it. Since, Yagu, I have flown a fair bit across Australia and internationally. I still don't enjoy flying but living in regional Western Australia means this is the quickest way. Every time I fly, I think of your words, and that you are always watching over me.

One of my favorite memories, flying into Geraldton in the 1970s and '80s, was the sight of Charlie and all his little kids waiting for me at the terminal. Seeing their smiling, welcoming faces. That is not possible anymore at the current airport with all the barriers and fences.

Yagu, you were right, flying was something to experience. It took me to places I never thought I would go. I saw the beauty of New Zealand's worm caves, thermal pools and green green lands. I flew over snow peaks between Calgary and Vancouver. I had never seen anything like that. I ate fine chocolates, touched snowflakes and spoke in the European Union in cold Brussels with sister Barbara. I flew straight across the Indian Ocean to South Africa and ate the most delicious tripe in Soweto. Above Uluru with its reds and purples reminded me of a beating heart, and the love of my people and country.

Venice, a movie set, travelling the Grand Canal with the gondolas gliding by. Living in a 500-year-old apartment and baking damper bread to share. In Manchester I tasted my first Scottish lobster, although I still prefer the Geraldton crayfish. On a flight to Abu Dhabi, I watched the longest sunset I have ever seen in my life – like you, it lasted forever.

Yagu, it has all been something to experience indeed.

WAJARRI GLOSSARY

aba	grandmother
abagurdany	your grandmother
bajarnmanha	being angry
bajayimanha	becoming angry
balygurr	bush broom
bardi	edible witchetty grub
bariya	path through bush/track
barna	ground, earth, country
barndimanmanha	making better, making stronger
barndijunmanha	putting it right
bibarlu	paper
bibarlu wangga	paper talk
biliyarra	red
bimba	tree gum
buwa	younger brother
dambamanmanha	making damper
gagurlimanha	leaving on own
gaja	offspring, child, daughter
gambu	cooked
gami	grandfather
gamigurdany	your grandfather
gantharri	grandmother
gudiya	one
gudurdu	heart
gurda	older brother
gurninyimanha	feeling sorry for someone
guru	eye
gurugilaaji	eye glasses
gutharra	two
guwiyarl	sand goanna
guwiyarl guga gambu	cooked goanna meat

jiibu bimbily	sheep flaps/ribs
jiibu bitharn	sheep liver
jiibu maga	sheep head
jiibu nyurililiny	sheep runners/intestines
jiibu nyurndi	sheep tails
jiibu thalba	sheep sweet bread/brain
jiibu warri	sheep tripe
jirdilungu	milky way
jirrararda	dust
jundanmanha	sweeping
jurnimanha	laughing
mama	father
mamagurdany	your father
-manha	present tense
mara	hand
maraji	aunty
marda	money
marlu guga gambu	red kangaroo meat, cooked
marlu nyurndi gambu	red kangaroo tail ,cooked
marn.gurr	three
mayu	child
migalgurnmanha	emptying out
mijiji	white woman
miyarnuwimanha	learning
mungaly-mungaly	evening, late afternoon
munggu	anthill
murdiyimanha	becoming cold winter
murnamayimanha	holding each other
nani gambu	goat, cooked or stewed
nani maga gambu	goat head, cooked
nganajungu	my, mine
nganajungu gami	my grandparents
nganajungu mama	my father
nganajungu winja	my old people

nganajungu yagu	my mother
nganggulangayiya	thinking about someone
ngurlumanmanha	scaring us
nganggunmanha	remembering
ngarlayigayimanha	looking around for something
ngarlbungga	the hot season
ngardunggayimanha	getting dark, night time
ngarlgu	bush onion
ngatha	I/me
nganggurnmanha	listening
-nha	past tense
nyarlu	woman/female
ruudu	road
thaga	coolamon
thana gagurlimanha	they separating, moving apart
wadjbellas	whitefellas
walgajunmanha	writing
wangga	talk
wanggajimanha	all talking together
wanggamanha	talking
warlarda	sandalwood
warlgu	quondongs
warlugura	teenage girl
warritharra	sorrow, pangs of unhappiness
warritharrayimanha	getting sad, unhappy
widara	long
winja nyarlu	old Aboriginal woman
winja yamaji	old Aboriginal man
yagu	mother
yagugurdany	your mother
yalibirri warla	emu egg
yalyba	four, more than three
yalyba guru	four eye
yamaji	Mid West Aboriginal person

BADIMAYA GLOSSARY

Badimaya	Mt Magnet/Paynes Find area
bagali	adult man
balu	he
bibi	mother
gadyardi	three
gami	grandparent, grandchild
gurriya	one
gudha	two
gudha-gudhara	four
gulu	house
gulydyirrabaya	getting hungry
mara gurriya	five
wangga	talking

ABORIGINAL ENGLISH GLOSSARY

nyorn   poor thing

unna   hey, don't you think, really

ACKNOWLEDGEMENTS

I would like to thank and acknowledge my two sons, Mark and Tamati, all of my extended family, friends colleagues – including Mick Adams, Juli Coffin, Neil Drew and Sandra Thompson – for their support in writing this book, and to cousin sister Debbie Green for language checking.

I would like to acknowledge Edith Cowan University, First Nation Australia Writers Network peers, The Lowitja Institute and Yamaji Art peers. Thank you to Kent MacCarter for his patience, commitment, editing and assistance. Some of the poems in this collection have previously appeared in *Cordite Poetry Review*, *The Kenyon Review* and *The Lifted Brow*. My thanks go out to the editors.

I also wish to acknowledge, regarding Indigenous language revitalisation and maintenance, the incredible work done in the Yamaji region by the Yamaji Languages Aboriginal Corporation and the Bundiyarra Irra Wangga Language Centre. Lastly, I would like to acknowledge the Yamaji barna of my family and Ancestors that holds me, including the Southern Yamaji country on which I write.

Charmaine Papertalk Green is from the Wajarri, Badimaya and Southern Yamaji peoples of Mid West Western Australia. She has lived and worked in rural Western Australia (Mid West and Pilbara) most of her life, and within the Aboriginal sector industry as a community agitator, artist/poet, community development practitioner and social sciences researcher.

Her poetry has appeared in *Antipodes*, *Artlink Magazine*, *Cordite Poetry Review*, *The Kenyon Review* and *The Lifted Brow*, as well as in the anthologies *The Fremantle Press Anthology of Western Australian Poetry*, *Inside Black Australia: An Anthology of Aboriginal Poetry*, *Ora Nui: A Collection of Maori and Aboriginal Literature*, *The Penguin Book of Australian Women Poets* and *Those Who Remain Will Always Remember: An Anthology of Aboriginal Writing*.

She lives in Geraldton, Western Australia.

Left: Charmaine Papertalk Green on the steps of Bentley Girls Hostel, 1978

73